CLASSIC AME FUNERAL VEHICLES 1900 THROUGH 1980
PHOTO ARCHIVE

Walt McCall & Tom McPherson

Iconografix
Photo Archive Series

Iconografix
PO Box 446
Hudson, Wisconsin 54016 USA

Iconografix books are offered at a discount when sold in quantity for promotional use. Businesses or organizations seeking details should write to the Marketing Department, Iconografix, at the above address.

Library of Congress Card Number: 99-76053

ISBN 1-58388-016-X

00 01 02 03 04 05 06 5 4 3 2 1

Printed in the United States of America

Cover and book design by Shawn Glidden

Copy editing by Dylan Frautschi

Iconografix Inc. exists to preserve history through the publication of notable photographic archives and the list of titles under the Iconografix imprint is constantly growing. Transportation enthusiasts should be on the Iconografix mailing list and are invited to write and ask for a catalog, free of charge.

Authors and editors in the field of transportation history are invited to contact the Editorial Department at Iconografix, Inc., PO Box 446, Hudson, WI 54016. We require a minimum of 120 photographs per subject. We prefer subjects narrow in focus, e.g., a specific model, railroad, or racing venue. Photographs must be of high-quality, suited to large format reproduction.

PREFACE

The histories of machines and mechanical gadgets are contained in the books, journals, correspondence, and personal papers stored in libraries and archives throughout the world. Written in tens of languages, covering thousands of subjects, the stories are recorded in millions of words.

Words are powerful. Yet, the impact of a single image, a photograph or an illustration, often relates more than dozens of pages of text. Fortunately, many of the libraries and archives that house the words also preserve the images.

In the *Photo Archive Series,* Iconografix reproduces photographs and illustrations selected from public and private collections. The images are chosen to tell a story—to capture the character of their subject. Reproduced as found, they are accompanied by the captions made available by the archive.

The Iconografix *Photo Archive Series* is dedicated to young and old alike, the enthusiast, the collector and anyone who, like us, is fascinated by "things" mechanical.

ACKNOWLEDGMENTS

Most of the photographs in this book came from the personal collection of Walter M.P. McCall. A significant number of these photos were acquired over the years from close personal friend and fellow professional car historian, Thomas A. McPherson. We are also grateful to Bernie DeWinter IV, Steven B. Loftin and Kent Roduck for their contributions to this project, and to The Professional Car Society, an international organization dedicated to the preservation and appreciation of antique and vintage funeral coaches, ambulances and related vehicles.

BIBLIOGRAPHY

McPherson, Thomas A., SUPERIOR: THE COMPLETE HISTORY, Specialty Vehicle Press, Don Mills, Ontario, Canada 1995.

McPherson, Thomas A., THE EUREKA COMPANY, A COMPLETE HISTORY, Specialty Vehicle Press, Don Mills, Ontario, Canada 1994.

McPherson, Thomas A., FLXIBLE PROFESSIONAL VEHICLES: THE COMPLETE HISTORY, Specialty Vehicle Press, Don Mills, Ontario, Canada 1993.

McPherson, Thomas A., AMERICAN FUNERAL CARS & AMBULANCES SINCE 1900, Crestline Publishing, Glen Ellyn, Illinois 1973.

McCall, Walter M.P., Editor - THE PROFESSIONAL CAR, quarterly publication of The Professional Car Society, Columbus, Ohio.

1900 SAYERS & SCOVILL HORSE-DRAWN HEARSE - This was the type of equipment the big-city undertaker was using at the turn of the century. Built by Sayers & Scovill of Cincinnati, OH, this premium horse-drawn hearse has an eight-column body with a combination of carved panels and plate glass, and a smooth "mosque deck" roof. Note the hammercloth-covered driver's seat and ornate coach lamps. Rubber-tired vehicles of this style were marketed as "funeral cars" - not hearses.

INTRODUCTION

Because they are discomforting reminders of our own mortality, hearses and other funeral service vehicles remain one of the most neglected chapters in American auto industry history.

Since its formation in 1976, the Professional Car Society - a historical and educational group dedicated to the preservation and appreciation of antique and vintage funeral cars and ambulances - has done much to improve this situation, but funeral vehicles still aren't universally welcome at antique auto shows. That's a pity, because hearses are the last bastion of true custom body design and coachcraft.

The American funeral car industry is a direct descendent of the carriage and buggy manufacturing trade. Some of the industry's best-known names - Henney, Eureka and A.J. Miller - were former buggy makers that switched to hearse and ambulance manufacturing as a matter of survival when the newfangled automobile replaced horse-drawn vehicles.

For much of this century hearse and ambulance manufacturing in the United States was centered in Ohio and Illinois. Most of the major players were in central and southern Ohio: Superior in Lima; A.J. Miller in Bellefontaine; Meteor in Piqua; Sayers & Scovill in Cincinnati, and Flxible in Loudonville. The two other major players - Henney and Eureka - were located in Freeport and Rock Falls, Illinois. A number of smaller hearse and ambulance companies (Barnette, Economy, Memphian, Weller Bros. and Pinner) thrived in Memphis, Tennessee.

The vehicles illustrated in this book include four basic types of professional cars. Most common is the processional hearse or funeral coach, which transported the casket in solemn dignity from the place of service to the cemetery. Special-purpose flower cars appeared in the mid-1930s and were popular with larger funeral homes into the 1970s. Behind the scenes toiled the "service" or "first-call" car, which transported the deceased from place of death to the mortuary and hauled caskets and other equipment, saving wear and tear on the funeral director's front-line hearse.

One of the industry's most popular offerings was the dual-purpose Combination Funeral Coach & Ambulance. This versatile vehicle could be quickly converted from a hearse to an emergency ambulance when needed, and vice-versa, saving the small-town undertaker the considerable cost of a second vehicle.

The ultra-conservative hearse industry utilized just three basic body styles through the entire 20th Century. For the first two decades, most hearses were of the columned, carved-panel style, which made the epic transition from horse to gasoline power.

In the mid-1920s, the tall, old-fashioned carved-drape hearse was succeeded by the long, low limousine style "Funeral Coach," which was designed to blend in with the other cars in the funeral procession. The ornamental carved-panel hearse made a dramatic comeback in the 1930s, but disappeared by the end of the Second World War. At first, these massive simulated draperies were carved out of solid wood, but later models had cast metal or stamped steel drapery panels to reduce vehicle weight. By far the most enduring of all 20th Century hearse body styles was the classic Landau, which appeared in the late 1930s. With its formal rear quarters and elegant carriage bows, the seemingly-timeless landau is basically the only body style offered by the North American funeral car industry today.

Up until the 1930s, hearse and ambulance bodies were mounted on lengthened passenger car chassis. Luxury makes were preferred for their upscale cachet, dependability and slow rate of depreciation. In 1935, Cadillac and Packard introduced special long-wheelbase chassis designed especially for hearse and ambulance builders. The "commercial chassis" was the backbone of the industry into the 1980s. Cadillac has dominated the professional car market in North America since the 1950s, but rival Lincoln has been encroaching on Cadillac's turf in recent years.

The most significant development in hearse design during the 20th Century was side-loading. Introduced in the late 1920s, the side-servicing hearse had a movable casket table, which swung out over the curb on either side of the car. With traditional rear loading through the back door, the "three-way" was the most desirable of all hearses - and the most expensive, especially when equipped with a power-operated casket table. The side-loading hearse came to the end of the line with auto industry downsizing in the late 1970s. The last three-way hearses were built in 1984.

Because they were meticulously maintained, carefully driven and rarely abused, many classic funeral vehicles survive today in the appreciative hands of funeral homes, antique auto collectors and members of the Professional Car Society. It is not uncommon to find a hundred or more passenger car-based hearses, ambulances and related vehicles at PCS meets around the country. The Society's address is PO Box 09636, Columbus, OH 43209.

1913 LEO GILLIG AUTOMOBILE HEARSE - Crane & Breed of Cincinnati, OH, introduced America's first factory-built automobile hearse in 1909. Rival James Cunningham & Son was close behind. Many early motor hearses consisted of former horse-drawn bodies remounted on lengthened passenger car chassis. The Leo Gillig Automobile Works of San Francisco built this eight-columned auto hearse with semi-open C-type cab. The chassis builder is unknown.

1914 CUNNINGHAM CARVED-PANEL HEARSE - This was the style of hearse which made the transition from horse to motor power. The eight-column design with carved wood drapery panels on the sides and rear was the dominant hearse style through the first two decades of the 1900s. This high, boxy style was supplanted by the long, low limousine hearse in the 1920s. This light gray carved hearse was built by the James Cunningham Son & Company of Rochester, NY, on the company's own Model "R" chassis.

1922 KNIGHTSTOWN-STUDEBAKER CHILD'S HEARSE - Many undertakers had small, white hearses for the funerals of children. This one, on a Studebaker Big Six chassis, was built by the Knightstown Body Company of Knightstown, IN. Owned by Dave Neitzel of Moorseville, IN, it was photographed at a Professional Car Society meet in Marietta, OH. Note the leaded glass "Angel Wings" design in the rear side windows. Happily, improved medicine and drastically reduced infant mortality rendered the pathetic Child's Hearse all but obsolete by 1950.

1925 EUREKA-REO LANDAU BACK LIMOUSINE HEARSE - The Eureka Company of Rock Falls, IL, introduced a bold, new hearse body style in the early 1920s. By the end of the decade the "limousine" style had all but replaced the tall, carved-panel hearse, which had dominated the industry since the turn of the century. This premium model limousine hearse has a padded leather rear roof ornamented with landau irons and oval opera windows. Note also the etched glass in the side windows.

1928 CUNNINGHAM CARVED-PANEL HEARSE - The ultra-conservative James Cunningham Son & Company of Rochester, NY, continued to offer eight-columned carved-panel hearses long after its competitors had abandoned this outdated style in favor of the limousine. This staid example sports huge drum headlights, periscope-style parking lights atop the front fenders, and disc wheels.

SAYERS & SCOVILL FACTORY, 1929 - This interesting photograph, taken outside the Sayers & Scovill plant in Cincinnati, OH, shows the dramatic progress in hearse design over a period of 40 years. At left is a small white horse-drawn child's hearse of the 1880s. The car on the right is the limited production S&S "Signed Sculpture" Town Car Hearse introduced on the eve of the Depression in 1929. Sayers & Scovill's "Signed Sculpture" hearse had large cast bronze "Angel of Memory" panels designed and signed by noted American sculptor Clement Barnhorn.

1930 SUPERIOR-STUDEBAKER BUCKINGHAM LIMOUSINE FUNERAL COACH - Founded as a bus builder in 1923, the Superior Body Company of Lima, OH, added hearses and ambulances to its product line in 1925. Superior had a close partnership with Studebaker well into the 1930s. This is a catalog illustration of Superior's top-line Buckingham Limousine Funeral Coach, which was built on an elongated Studebaker President chassis. Note the gracefully curved roofline with integral windshield visor, draped windows, and the wooden flower trays visible through the rear side windows.

1931 FLXIBLE-BUICK SIDE-SERVICING HEARSE - The most important development in hearse design to come out of the 1920s was side-loading. The Eureka Company of Rock Falls, IL, and the John W. Henney Company of Freeport, IL, introduced side-loading hearses almost simultaneously in 1926-1927. This feature, which consisted of a moveable casket table that swung out over the curb through double doors on each side of the car, was an industry staple for more than 60 years. Side-servicing was a victim of federally mandated vehicle "downsizing" in the late 1970s.

1932 SUPERIOR-CADILLAC TOWN CAR FUNERAL COACH - American funeral coach styling reached its zenith in the classic era of the 1930s. Inspired by the formal luxury cars of the day, funeral car manufacturers also offered open-front town car hearses and ambulances. This one, on a 1932 Cadillac V-8 Series 355-B chassis, was built by the Superior Body Company of Lima, OH. A tonneau roof buttoned into place over the open chauffeur's compartment in inclement weather. A full-length flower tray is visible through the draped rear windows.

1933 CUNNINGHAM "SILVER CATHEDRAL" CARVED TOWN CAR HEARSE - Founded in 1838, James Cunningham & Son Company was one of America's premium carriage builders. The Rochester, NY, company was also well-known for its high quality, very expensive hearses and ambulances. Cunningham built this stunning eight column carved town car hearse on its own W-1 chassis for A.R. Orlowski of Buffalo, NY. A victim of the Depression, Cunningham ceased vehicle production in 1936 - two years short of what would have been its centennial.

1934 HENNEY PIERCE-ARROW "ARROWLINE" LIMOUSINE HEARSE - Formerly a major buggy maker, the John W. Henney Company of Freeport, IL, started building motor hearses and ambulances in 1916. The Henney Motor Company of Freeport, IL, quickly became one of the industry's leaders. From 1934 through 1937, Henney offered limited production premium hearses and ambulances on Pierce-Arrow chassis. Mike Reifer of Owensville, MO, restored this rare 1934 Henney Arrowline which was photographed at the 1998 Professional Car Society International Meet in Chicago, IL.

1935 SUPERIOR STUDEBAKER ELMHURST SERVICE CAR - The service car was the workhorse of the funeral home fleet. Also known as a "first-call" car, the Service Car removed the deceased from the home or hospital to the funeral parlor. It also transported caskets, chairs and other equipment, saving wear and tear on the funeral director's front-line processional hearse. Superior's hard-working Elmhurst Service Car was powered by Studebaker's Dictator Six engine.

1935 HENNEY-PACKARD ONE-TWENTY LIMOUSINE HEARSE - In 1935, Packard introduced a long-wheelbase commercial chassis version of its new, moderately-priced One-Twenty. Designed especially for mounting hearse and ambulance bodies, the new 120A Commercial Chassis was a huge hit with American hearse and ambulance builders. This 1935 Henney-Packard Model 800 Nu-3-Way Side-Servicing Limousine Funeral Coach was photographed at the gates of the Packard Proving Grounds near Utica, MI.

20

1935 MILLER-CHRYSLER "ART MODEL" FUNERAL COACH - In 1934 the A.J. Miller Company of Bellefontaine, OH, introduced a new funeral car body style which combined the graceful arches of a carved-panel hearse with the sleek lines of a limousine. Built through 1937, Miller's "Art Models" featured beveled glass above the beltline within the arch. Miller Art Models were built on a wide variety of chassis, including this 1935 Chrysler Airstream. This impressive Miller-Chrysler Art Model is owned by Dale Schmidt of Nazareth, PA.

1936 SIEBERT-FORD ARISTOCRAT LIMOUSINE FUNERAL CAR - The Shop of Siebert Associates of Toledo, OH, offered a line of economy model hearse, ambulance, combination, and service car conversions based on stretched Ford V-8s from 1933 through the mid-1950s, and from 1960-1964. Siebert's top-line models were called Siebert Aristocrats. The Seagle Funeral Home of Pulaski, VA, was the original purchaser of this 1936 Siebert-Ford, which Oscar Seagle had professionally restored in the early 1990s.

CAD. 4724-3

1937 METEOR-LaSALLE FLOWER CARS - A new type of vehicle was introduced to the funeral profession in the late 1930s. It was the Flower Car which was designed to lead the funeral procession, impressively banked with the funeral flowers. Prior to Eureka's introduction of this genre in 1936, touring cars or phaetons with their tops let down were used for this purpose. Flower cars soon became an important part of every large funeral firm's fleet. Delivered to a New York livery, these Meteor-LaSalle Flower Cars have dummy convertible tops and rear boots, and open, canvas-lined flower wells.

1938 FLXIBLE-CADILLAC CARVED-DRAPE HEARSE - Originally a manufacturer of motorcycle sidecars, The Flxible Company of Loudonville, OH, later switched to building buses. The company entered the funeral coach and ambulance field in 1925. From the start, Flxible enjoyed a close working relationship with the Buick Motor Division of General Motors, but between 1938 and 1942 built small numbers of professional cars on Cadillac chassis. This imposing carved-drape hearse was built with the 160-inch wheelbase Cadillac Series 75 commercial chassis.

1938 FLXIBLE-BUICK "CLASSIC A" CARVED-DRAPE HEARSE - In 1938, Flxible added a distinctly different style of carved hearse to its product line. It was the "Classic A," which featured carved imitation drapes set into arched side windows with complementing ornamental trim between the arches and below the belt line. This model was also available in a "Classic AA" version, which had conventional window glass in the arches. Flxible's Classic A and AA models were built on Buick, LaSalle, and Cadillac chassis through 1942.

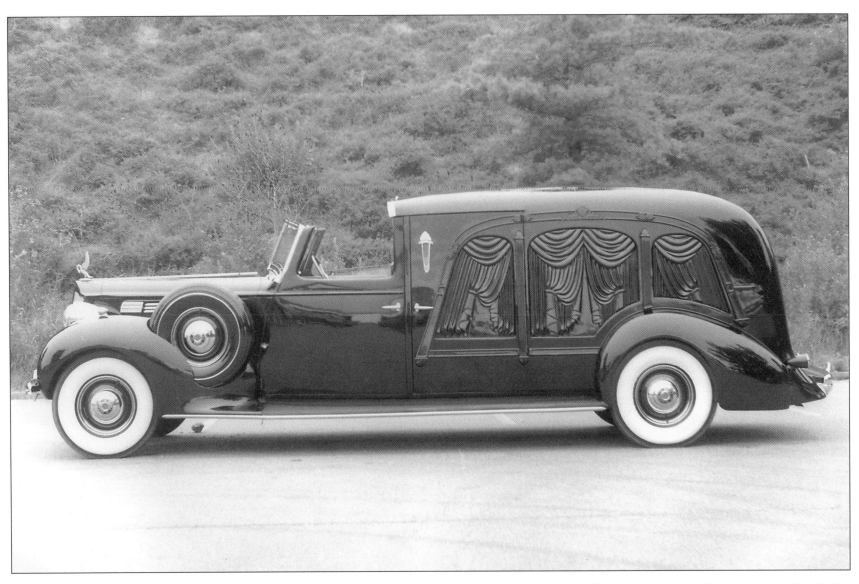

1938 MILLER-PACKARD CARVED TOWN CAR HEARSE - This classic open-front town car hearse marked the height of style in American funeral coach design. Built by the A.J. Miller Company of Bellefontaine, OH, on the 1938 Packard commercial chassis, it features three richly-carved simulated drape panels within a graceful arch on each side of the car; ornamental coach lamps, open chauffeur's compartment, and a chrome-plated, V-type windshield. This imposing hearse is owned by funeral director William Peoples of Marietta, OH.

1938 HENNEY-PACKARD MODEL 886A FLOWER CAR - The Henney Motor Company added a long-wheelbase flower car to its product line for 1938. Built on the Packard commercial chassis, Henney's flower car featured a simulated convertible coupe roof, a convertible-type boot at the rear of the car, and an adjustable flower deck. A compartment below the flower deck was large enough to accommodate a cot or casket, greatly increasing this vehicle's utility. This 1938 Henney-Packard Flower Car was restored by funeral director Mahlon M. Thompson of Cranbury, NJ.

1939 BRANTFORD/HENNEY-CADILLAC "FORMAL" LIMOUSINE HEARSE - Henney steadfastly refused to build a carved-panel hearse. Henney's answer to the carved-drape cars sold by its competitors was the "Formal Model," which featured large art deco panels on each side and the rear door of the car. The Henney Formal was offered from 1938-1940. In Canada, Henney hearses and ambulances were built under licence by Brantford Coach & Body of Brantford, Ontario. The Packard-exclusive deal signed by Henney in 1937 didn't apply in Canada, resulting in Henney-Cadillacs and LaSalles as well as Henney-Packards.

1940 SUPERIOR-CADILLAC TARRYTOWN CARVED HEARSE - The artistic carved-drape hearse made a dramatic comeback during the 1930s, but was on the decline as the 1940s began. The Superior Coach Corporation introduced this new carved-drape style in 1939. Note the escutcheon on the front door and the hinging for the massive rear side door. Somebody forgot to close the Cadillac "Flying Goddess" hood latch when this photo was taken.

1940 MILLER-OLDSMOBILE GOTHIC-PANEL CARVED HEARSE - The A. J. Miller Company introduced a fresh, new carved hearse style in 1939. A.J. Miller's new design featured three freestanding gothic panels on each side of the car and two more on the rear door. Miller's new Cathedral type carved body was available on Cadillac, LaSalle, Oldsmobile, and Buick chassis. Miller offered its customers both gothic panel and carved drape hearses through 1942.

1941 METEOR-CADILLAC GOTHIC-PANEL CARVED HEARSE - The Meteor Motor Car Company of Piqua, OH, was a major player in the U.S. funeral coach and ambulance industry from 1917 until it merged with A.J. Miller to form Miller-Meteor in 1956. Meteor introduced this new carved hearse design in 1939. Less ornate than the full-draped style, Meteor's Cathedral Style hearse featured three gothic window panels, complete with filigree trim and carved columns. The side door is hinged in the center of the wide middle window.

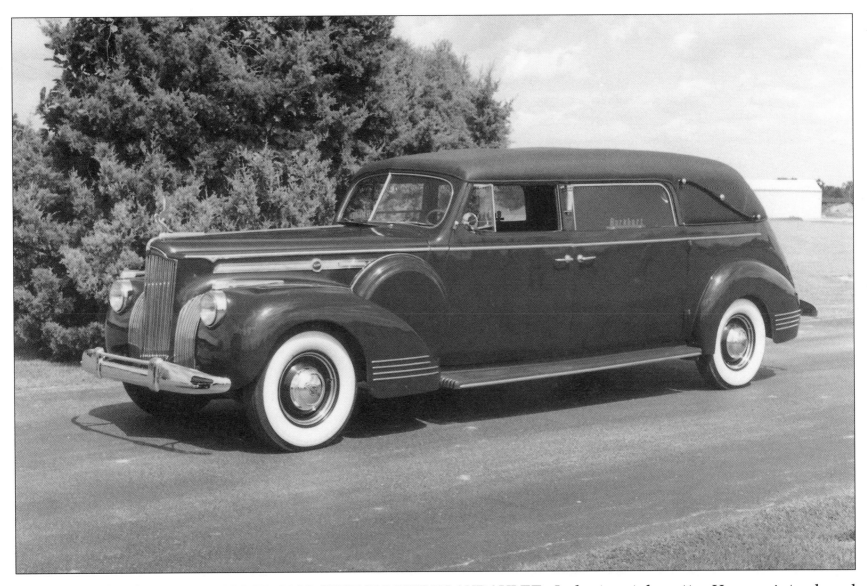

1941 HENNEY-PACKARD MODEL 4198 CUSTOM-BUILT LANDAULET - Industry style-setter Henney introduced a new premium model hearse called the Custom-Built Landaulet in 1938. This limited production model with special low roofline, formal landau styling, and drapeless side windows was offered through 1942. The Custom-Built Landaulet was also available in open-front Town Car and side-servicing versions. This fine example is owned by Michael Burkhart of Dodge City, KS.

1941 HENNEY-PACKARD MODEL 4102 LANDAULET FUNERAL COACH - Sayers & Scovill popularized a new funeral coach body style - the landau - in 1938. Within a few years the stately landau become the industry's most popular body style. The classic landau continues to dominate the industry to this day, more than six decades later. Henney introduced a "metal back" landau with smooth roof for 1941. This nicely restored example is owned by Robert Hassebroeck of Sullivan, MO.

1942 FLXIBLE-CADILLAC "INNOVATION"- Flxible introduced one of the industry's most daring departures in funeral car design for 1942. The Flxible Innovation offered the sleek styling of a coupe-type flower car, but with a smooth, rounded rear deck that was not intended to carry flowers. The Innovation's sides were ornamented with carved columns and an urn motif. Flxible built two Cadillacs and two Buicks of this style, but World War II intervened and the Innovation was nowhere to be found when Flxible resumed professional car production in 1945.

1946 EUREKA-CADILLAC LANDAU FUNERAL COACH - Funeral car and ambulance manufacturers were hard pressed to meet pent-up demand for new vehicles when professional car production resumed after the war. Virtually all of the industry's 1946 offerings were warmed-over versions of prewar models. The formal landau body style had taken over where the carved-panel hearse had left off. This 1946 Eureka-Cadillac Landau sports a smooth painted roof, stately landau irons and coach lamps.

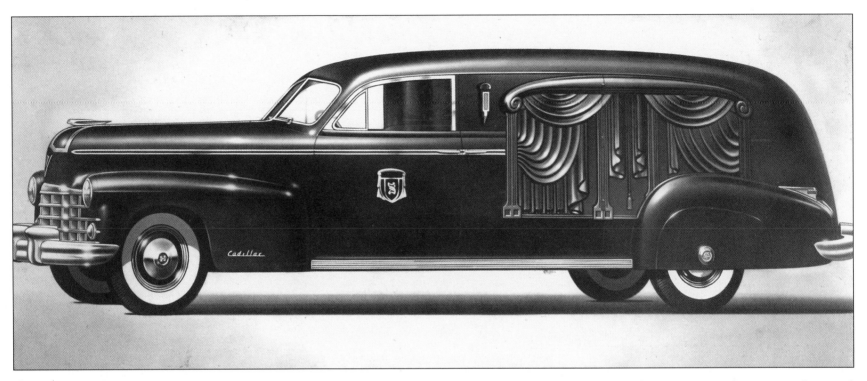

1947 SAYERS & SCOVILL CADILLAC CARVED MACEDONIAN - Replaced by the limousine, the carved-panel hearse made a dramatic comeback in 1934. With the notable exception of Henney, all U.S. hearse manufacturers added carved-panel hearses to their model lines, but this renaissance was relatively brief. The carved hearse was just as quickly succeeded by the new landau body style in the early 1940s. When funeral car production resumed after World War II, the carved-drape hearse had all but disappeared. Only conservative S&S included a carved-drape hearse in its postwar advertising. Originally introduced in 1941, Sayers & Scovill's Macedonian carved hearse was offered through 1947. Very few were sold.

1948 S&S CADILLAC VICTORIA LANDAU FUNERAL COACH - After its acquisition of Sayers & Scovill in 1945, the Hess & Eisenhardt Company of Cincinnati, OH, continued to market its products under the S&S name. The S&S Cadillac Victoria was H&E's best known product from its introduction in 1938 through the sale of the company to Superior in 1981. S&S/Superior Coaches of Lima, OH, continues to use the Victoria name to this day. Note the padded leather roof and distinctive S&S chrome trim on the nose of this stately side-servicing hearse built for Stine & McClure of Kansas City, MO.

1949 S&S CADILLAC CARVED-PANEL HEARSE - The ornate carved-panel hearse enjoyed a spectacular renaissance from 1934 through 1942, when it was succeeded by the formal landau body style. Very few carved-drape hearses were built after the Second World War. Hess & Eisenhardt built a small number of limousine style S&S Cadillac hearses and service cars with carved-panel window inserts between 1946 and 1950. This one is mounted on the all-new 1949 Cadillac Series 86 commercial chassis.

1949 FLXIBLE-BUICK LANDAU FUNERAL COACH - The Flxible Company introduced its first all-new postwar models for 1949. The totally redesigned 1949 Flxibles were built on Buick chassis exclusively. All featured dramatically long, low styling. This is the 1949 Flxible Premier Landaulet on Buick Roadmaster chassis. Note the distinctive Buick "ventiports" in the front fenders - four on the top-line Premier and three on the less expensive Flxible Sterling series.

1950 SUPERIOR-CADILLAC LANDAULET - Two body styles - the classic limousine and formal landau - now dominated the U.S. funeral car industry. Cadillac's 158-inch wheelbase Series 86 commercial chassis was sold to five funeral car and ambulance manufacturers — Superior Coach of Lima, OH; Hess & Eisenhardt (S&S) of Cincinnati, OH; A.J. Miller, Bellefontaine, OH; the Meteor Motor Car Company of Piqua, OH; and The Eureka Company of Rock Falls, IL. This formal 1950 Superior-Cadillac has an optional padded leather roof and white sidewall tires.

1950 SUPERIOR-CADILLAC COUPE DE FLEUR FLOWER CAR - The Flower Car reached the peak of its popularity in the 1950s. No funeral home fleet could be considered complete without one. Flower cars were standard offerings in every major funeral car manufacturer's product line. Superior Coach called its Cadillac flower car the Coupe de Fleur - a name which would continue for the next 11 years. This white 1950 Superior-Cadillac Coupe de Fleur features the wraparound rear window from a Cadillac coupe and a hydraulically-adjustable, stainless steel flower deck.

1950 MILLER-CADILLAC LANDAU FUNERAL COACH - A distinctive styling feature of the landau hearses built by the A.J. Miller Company between 1949 and 1956 was the angled oval window between the rear side door and the chrome-plated landau bow. This was a delete option which could be left off if desired. The vast majority of Miller's customers requested this distinctive feature. This is the 1950 Miller-Cadillac End Loading Landau.

1950 HENNEY-PACKARD MODEL 15096 FLOWER CAR - The Henney Motor Company did not resume postwar hearse and ambulance production until the 1948 model year. Henney's 22nd Series (1948) and 23rd Series (1949-1950) models were the most successful in the company's history. Banked with flowers at a PCS meet, this remarkably original 1950 Henney-Packard Flower Car is owned by nationally-known Packard historian George L. Hamlin of Clarksville, MD.

Custom Built DESIGNED AND BUILT BY THE EUREKA COMPANY (INC.1887) ROCK FALLS, ILLINOIS 1951

1252-C

1951 EUREKA-CADILLAC LANDAU FUNERAL COACH - The Eureka Company of Rock Falls, IL was known for its lavishly-appointed funeral coach interiors and three-way casket tables. This is a rear view of a standard Eureka-Cadillac Three-Way Landau. Note the large ornamental sidelamp between the rear door and the upper end of the landau bow - a trademark of Eureka's landau hearses from 1947 through 1959.

44

1951 METEOR-CADILLAC FLOWER CAR - Coupe style flower cars were standard offerings in every major funeral car and ambulance manufacturer's product lines. Each had its own distinctive coupe style. Meteor used the entire "greenhouse" of the 1951 Cadillac coupe. This one was built for the Wellman's Funeral Home. Note the remote control spotlight mounted on the left windshield pillar, which indicates that this car was also used for first-call work.

1952 METEOR-CADILLAC LANDAU FUNERAL COACH - This striking two-tone landau hearse was built by the Meteor Motor Car Company of Piqua, OH. The lower body is finished in light metallic gray, the top gloss black. The large coach lamp mounted on the front door was a Meteor styling trademark from 1941 through 1953. Note also the unique paint treatment on the rear quarter panel behind the side door. This coach was a standard end-loader.

1952 FLXIBLE-BUICK PREMIER COMBINATION FUNERAL COACH/AMBULANCE - The Combination Coach was an important part of every funeral car and ambulance maker's product lineup. The dual-purpose Combination could be quickly converted from a hearse to an ambulance. Conversion equipment included folding attendant seats, cot locks, removable warning lights, and "Ambulance" window signs. Flxible ceased hearse and ambulance production at the end of the 1952 model year, but returned to the professional car field in 1959.

1953 SUPERIOR-CADILLAC SIDE-SERVICING LANDAULET FUNERAL COACH - Superior's most prestigious offering was the regal side-servicing landaulet with power operated casket table. At the touch of a button, the casket table would glide out either side of the car or through the rear door. This well-dressed Side-Servicing Landaulet has a black crinkle-finish roof and white sidewall tires. This would be the fourth and final year for this style of Cadillac's Series 86 commercial chassis.

1954 METEOR-CADILLAC LIMOUSINE FUNERAL COACH - Funeral car styling closely followed that of the auto industry. Styling features such as wraparound windshields and rear quarter windows were incorporated into next-generation funeral cars and ambulances as fast as Detroit introduced them. This 1954 Meteor limousine hearse is a good example. Hess & Eisenhardt (S&S) introduced rear quarter windows in 1953. Within a year, everybody offered them. This coach is also equipped with modern "airline" type window drapes.

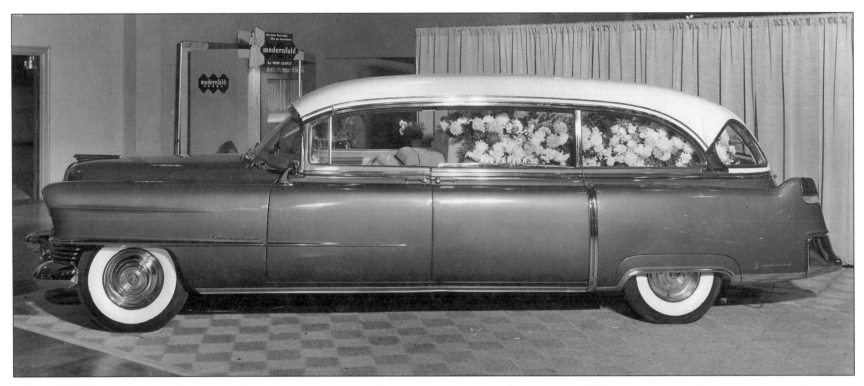

1954 SUPERIOR-CADILLAC BEAU MONDE FLORAL HEARSE - In 1954, Superior announced a pillarless hardtop-style professional car series called the Beau Monde. This was the prototype. The Beau Monde was offered in Floral Hearse, Flower Car and Combination versions in the 1955-1956 model years. The casket was carried under a rear compartment mound on which the funeral flowers were displayed. This car's most distinctive styling feature was its sweeping roofline and huge expanse of glass.

1954 SUPERIOR-CADILLAC COUPE DE FLEUR FLOWER CAR - Superior-Cadillac flower cars built between 1954 and 1956 utilized this curvaceous coupe-style cab, which utilized Cadillac's wraparound rear window. Except when banked with flowers, rearward visibility was excellent for this kind of car. The stainless steel flower deck could be hydraulically adjusted to artistically arrange floral sprays and baskets.

1954 SUPERIOR-PONTIAC LANDAULET FUNERAL COACH - In addition to its pricey Cadillacs, Superior offered a lower priced companion line of hearses, ambulances, service cars and combinations on a stretched Pontiac Bonneville chassis. Superior-Pontiacs were offered from 1936-1942; 1946-1948 and from 1953 through the 1975 model year. Two Superior-Pontiac funeral coach body styles were offered - the stylish landaulet shown here (with optional crinkle-finish roof) and the classic limousine.

1954 HENNEY-PACKARD LANDAULET FUNERAL COACH - This was the last year for the Henney-Packard. Henney won exclusive rights to the Packard commercial chassis in 1937, but the Freeport, IL, company was doomed to extinction along with the once-mighty Packard. Financially ailing Packard did not include a commercial chassis in its all-new 1955 product line, and Henney was forced out of business at the end of the 1954 model year. Henney introduced this attractive Richard Arbib styling for the 1951 model year.

1955 METEOR-CADILLAC LANDAULET FUNERAL COACH - Several funeral car manufacturers abandoned valance type window draperies for more practical, less formal "airline style" drapes. Patterned after those used in airliners, these drapes hung on top and bottom rods and could be quickly and easily closed for privacy. Airline type draperies were especially popular in combination coaches. Note how neatly the landau bow is integrated with the chrome upper side window trim.

1955 SUPERIOR-CADILLAC MODEL 604 SERVICE CAR - By the mid-fifties, the full sized luxury-type service car had become a rarity. Small vans and station wagons took over service car duties at funeral homes large and small. Some larger firms, however, insisted on nothing but the best regardless of cost. This 1955 Superior-Cadillac Service Car was built for the Snellings Funeral Home. The stylized chrome wreath ornament and dual chrome streamers were standard Superior service car trim from 1949 well into the 1960s.

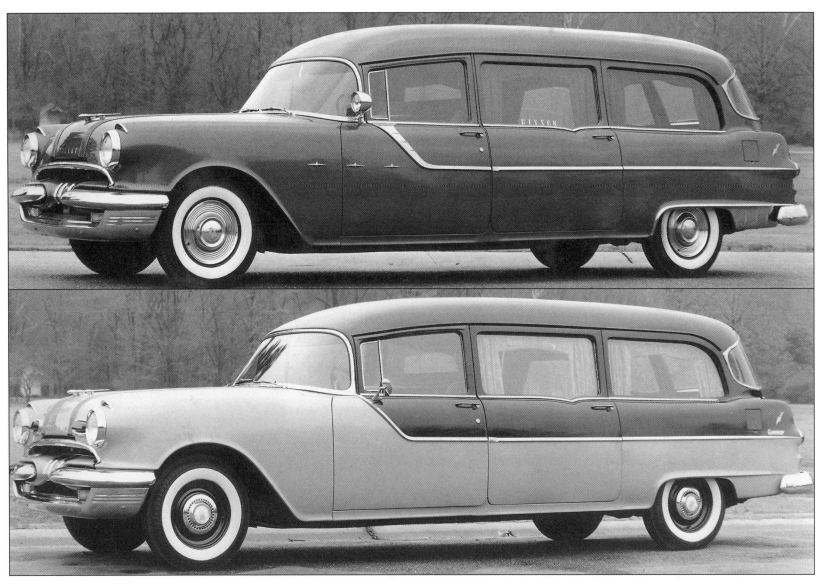

1955 ECONOMY/MEMPHIAN-PONTIAC LIMOUSINE COMBINATIONS - In addition to the major players, a number of smaller manufacturers were doing a brisk business building funeral cars and ambulances on lower-priced chassis such as Pontiac. These companies included Economy, Memphian, Comet, National, Barnette, Weller, Pinner, and Acme. The car at the top was built by Economy, which later changed its name to Memphian. The car at the bottom is a Memphian/Pontiac.

1956 S&S CADILLAC SUPERLINE KNICKERBOCKER CASKET CAR - Hess & Eisenhardt used some colorful names to identify its products. The Superline Knickerbocker Casket Car shown here is a case in point. H&E limousine hearses and combinations of the 1950s were invariably fitted with airline style drapes. Note the wraparound rear quarter windows and the exposed door hinges visible ahead of the vertical rear fender trim.

1956 S&S CADILLAC SUPERLINE FLORENTINE FLOWER CAR - Hess & Eisenhardt marketed its coupe-style flower cars as S&S Florentines. This 1956 S&S Superline Florentine has no rear side doors. Note the low coupe roof with large quarter panels, door-mounted nameplates, and the canvas cover buttoned neatly into place over the stainless steel flower deck.

L356/876

1956 SUPERIOR-CADILLAC LANDAULET - This formally-attired three-way hearse was built for the Jos. W. Bliley Company of Memphis, TN. Superior Coach used the side trim shown here for the 1954-1955-1956 model years. This landau is fitted with non-standard fringed drapes. The smooth roof is painted black, and the car has black sidewall tires. Note the chrome trim extended to the rear side doors.

1957 MEMPHIAN-CHRYSLER NEW YORKER LANDAU FUNERAL COACH - Smaller builders like Memphian and National offered hearses, ambulances and combinations built on any chassis desired by the customer. This handsome Memphian-Chrysler is a good example. Note the raised roofline, the large Eureka-style coach lamps mounted on the upper rear quarter panel, and the Memphian nameplate on the front fender.

1957 NATIONAL-IMPERIAL LANDAU FUNERAL COACH - Like Memphian, the National Body Manufacturing Company of Knightstown, IN, also built funeral coaches and ambulances on virtually any chassis desired by the purchaser. Professional cars built on Chrysler Imperial chassis were exceedingly rare. This Imperial landau hearse was built for the House of Diggs, a large Detroit funeral home chain. Note the large House of Diggs crest on the front and rear doors.

1957 COMET-OLDSMOBILE LIMOUSINE COMBINATION - The Comet Coach Company of Blytheville, AR, built this attractive two-tone Combination Funeral Coach and Ambulance on a stretched Oldsmobile chassis. Although they built on other makes on request, most of Comet's professional cars were Oldsmobiles. Comet sold its name to the Ford Motor Company in 1959 and was renamed the Cotner/Bevington Corporation after its two founders. Miller-Meteor later acquired Cotner/Bevington.

1957 SUPERIOR-CADILLAC MODERNE LANDAULET - Superior Coach dramatically restyled all of its professional cars for the 1957 model year. The bold, new look featured Superior's fresh new "Beau Monde" styling, which emphasized thin, sweeping rooflines and large glass areas. Note how the side doors extend into the roof panel on this handsome Moderne Side-Servicing Landaulet.

1957 SUPERIOR-CADILLAC COUPE DE FLEUR - For a funeral vehicle, Superior's all new 1957 Cadillac Coupe de Fleur Flower Car was downright sporty! This impressive example sports Superior's new reverse-slanted cab roof with "V" emblem and extruded aluminum trim on the lower rear quarter panels. The stainless steel deck could be hydraulically lowered or raised to accommodate various flower arrangements.

1957 S&S CADILLAC PARK PLACE COMBINATION HEARSE & FLOWER CAR - One of the most unique funeral vehicles built in the 1950s was Hess & Eisenhardt's Park Place, only a few of which were built during the 1957 and 1958 model years. Advertised as a combination hearse, flower and service car, the Park Place's rear roof folded down to form an open flower deck. With the top up the Park Place looked like a conventional landau hearse without landau bars. Shown here configured as a Flower Car, this Park Place was delivered to the Spitler Funeral home in Montoursville, PA.

581000-2

1958 S&S CADILLAC SUPERLINE KNICKERBOCKER CASKET CAR - Hess & Eisenhardt used some upscale names to identify its products - Knickerbocker, Park Row, Park Hill, Park Place, etc. This is a classic S&S Cadillac end-loading limousine funeral coach. Note the distinctive S&S body side moldings and the airline style draperies, which were standard on S&S funeral coaches from 1954 through the 1960s.

L3573410

1958 SUPERIOR-CADILLAC LANDAULET COMBINATION - Most combinations were of the limousine body style, but some funeral homes, which could afford only one coach for both funeral and ambulance service, preferred the formal look of the classic landau. This Landaulet Combination has the usual airline-style window drapes.

1958 MILLER-METEOR CADILLAC FLOWER CAR - In late 1956, the A.J. Miller Company and Meteor Motor Car Company were merged to form a new entity called Miller-Meteor. The first Miller-Meteors, built in the former Miller plant in Bellefontaine, OH, were introduced for the 1957 model year. This sparkling white Miller-Meteor Cadillac Flower Car was photographed in a studio setting. Note the owner's initial emblem on the rear side door.

1959 SUPERIOR-CADILLAC CROWN ROYALE LANDAULET - Superior dramatically restyled all of its professional cars for the 1959 model year. For the first time, two distinct series of Cadillac funeral coaches and ambulances were offered - Royale and Crown Royale. Styling of Superior's top-line Crown Royale Landaulet was nothing less than spectacular. A heavy chrome molding encircled the rear roof area and the new landau bow was almost straight. The rear roof area had a crinkle finish.

1959 SUPERIOR-CADILLAC ROYALE COUPE DE FLEUR - Funeral coach and ambulance manufacturers faced a major challenge designing dignified bodies for the flamboyant 1959 Cadillac commercial chassis with its towering rocketship tail fins. Superior matched this flashy chassis with equally dramatic body styling. One of the most stunning was the company's coupe style flower car. Note the nameplates mounted on the door and the aluminum trim on the lower rear fenders.

1959 MILLER-METEOR CADILLAC FUTURA LIMOUSINE COMBINATION - Most of Superior's competitors opted for more conservative styling on the flashy 1959 Cadillac commercial chassis. This Miller-Meteor Futura Limousine features two-tone paint on the fins and lower roof area. Note the crucifix in the rear side door window and the folding attendant's seat visible in the rear, which clearly indicate that this is a dual-purpose combination funeral coach/ambulance.

1959 EUREKA-CADILLAC SIDE-SERVICING LIMOUSINE FUNERAL COACH - The Eureka Company finally made the switch to all-steel body construction in 1957. Eureka's limousine style bodies featured attractively angled "C" and "D" pillars, with complementing "D" pillar chrome trim. This formal electric side-servicing hearse wears full-formal draperies.

1959 FLXIBLE-BUICK PREMIER LIMOUSINE FUNERAL COACH - After an absence of seven years, the Flxible Company resumed hearse and ambulance production in its plant in Loudonville, OH, for the 1959 model year. Flxible offered two series of coaches - the standard-wheelbase Flxette and the long-wheelbase Premier. Flxible again built exclusively on Buick chassis. The bat-winged 1959 Buick made an attractive base for Flxible's long-wheelbase Premier Limousine Funeral Coach.

1960 SUPERIOR-CADILLAC CROWN ROYALE LANDAULET FUNERAL COACH - Cadillac softened its styling for the 1960 model year. The new look included more restrained tail fins and less chrome, especially in the grille area. Superior's top-line hearse was still the Crown Royale Landaulet with its distinctive up-and-over roof molding. Note the new swag-type window drapes and extruded aluminum rear fender applique.

1960 FLXIBLE-BUICK FLXETTE LIMOUSINE FUNERAL COACH - Flxible found an eager market for its short-wheelbase Flxette models, which were available in limousine and landau funeral coach, ambulance, combination, and service car versions. The moderately priced Flxette offered the economy and handling ease of a standard wheelbase passenger car with the raised roof interior roominess of a full-sized professional car.

1961 SUPERIOR-CADILLAC CROWN ROYALE LIMOUSINE COMBINATION - Superior Coach offered no fewer than four series of professional cars for 1961. In addition to the Royale and Crown Royale introduced in 1959, new Sovereign and Crown Sovereign models were added for 1961. Styling was again all-new. Crown Royale and Crown Sovereign models had up-and-over rear roof moldings. The rear roof area had a crinkle finish - the front section was smooth.

1961 SUPERIOR-CADILLAC ROYALE FLOWER CAR - The long, low Flower Car remained the most impressive model in Superior's comprehensive model lineup. A stainless steel compartment under the adjustable flower deck permitted the Coupe de Fleur to be used as a first-call or casket transfer vehicle. But the Flower Car was at its impressive best leading the funeral cortege to the church or cemetery. This 1961 Superior-Cadillac Royale Flower Car was painted gold with a white top. The owner's nameplates (Southern) were mounted on the front doors.

1961 MILLER-METEOR CADILLAC FUTURA LIMOUSINE COMBINATION - With its sweeping expanse of glass all around the car, the Futura Limousine was certainly aptly named. Owned by Cameron and Erma Maine of Dover, OH, this well-dressed 1961 Miller-Meteor Cadillac Combination was a familiar sight at Professional Car Society meets - including the very first one held in Cincinnati, OH, in 1977.

1961 FLXIBLE-BUICK PREMIER LANDAU FUNERAL COACH - The Flxible Company offered its customers a choice of two landau body styles. In addition to the standard Flxible Landau, the company offered a landau with rear quarter windows. This is a straight end-loading hearse. Note the airline type drapes and the extruded aluminum moldings over the side windows and accent panel. This styling was also available on the short-wheelbase Flxible Flxette.

1961 EUREKA-CADILLAC LANDAU FUNERAL COACHES - Officials of The Eureka Company hand over the keys to a fleet of four 1961 Eureka-Cadillac Landau Funeral Coaches in Eureka's hometown of Rock Falls, IL. Many customers preferred to pick up their new funeral coaches and ambulances at the factory and drive them home. This church was a popular location for the Eureka photographer.

1962 SUPERIOR-CADILLAC CROWN SOVEREIGN BROUGHAM - Introduced for 1961, the Crown Sovereign Brougham eclipsed the Crown Royale as Superior's most prestigious - and expensive - funeral coach. The stately Crown Sovereign used the same up-and-over roof molding as the less expensive Crown Royale, but had formal, closed quarter panels and special Crown Sovereign ornamentation on the back door.

1962 SUPERIOR-CADILLAC CROWN ROYALE LIMOUSINE COMBINATION - Superior's distinctive Crown Royale styling was also available on limousine funeral coaches and combinations. This 1962 Crown Royale Limousine has swag type draperies, full-length skeg moldings, and chrome rocker panel moldings. The rear doors are hinged on the B-pillar, as was the practice on most combination coaches.

1962 SUPERIOR-PONTIAC CONSORT LANDAU FUNERAL COACH - In mid-1961 Superior announced a new short-wheelbase Consort series. Built on a Pontiac Bonneville chassis with a raised roof, the Consort was Superior's response to Flxible's Flxette and standard wheelbase Oldsmobile, Pontiac, and Chevrolet conversions from Cotner/Bevington. The new Superior-Pontiac Consort was available in funeral coach, ambulance, combination, and funeral service car versions.

1963 SUPERIOR-CADILLAC SOVEREIGN SIDE-SERVICING LANDAULET - Threeway side-servicing was a popular option on top-line Cadillac hearses built by all of the major U.S. funeral coach manufacturers - Superior, S&S, Miller-Meteor, and Eureka. The casket table extended out either side of the car, as well as the rear door. In addition to the standard manually operated table, a power-operated casket table was also optionally available.

1963 SUPERIOR-CADILLAC SOVEREIGN LIMOUSINE COMBINATION - Superior's freshened 1963 model styling featured softly rounded rooflines with a distinctly formal look. The rear roof area of this Sovereign Limousine Combination was not unlike that of the top-line Crown Sovereign Brougham. The air scoop on the rear fender indicates that this was an air-conditioned unit.

1963 FLXIBLE-BUICK FLXETTE SERVICE CAR - Factory-built funeral service cars were becoming increasingly rare. Only a handful were being built annually between all of the major funeral car manufacturers. This short-wheelbase Flxible-Buick service car was built for the Martin L. Myers Funeral Home. The blanked-out side windows, wreath ornament, and chrome streamers were traditional funeral service car trim.

8390

1964 EUREKA-CADILLAC LANDAU HEARSE - This was the final year for The Eureka Company, which closed the doors of its Rock Falls, IL, plant at the end of the 1964 model year. Eureka's roots extended all the way back to 1887 when the company began as a furniture maker. But Eureka went out in real style, as the above photo attests. This straight end-loading hearse has a smooth, painted roof.

1964 SUPERIOR-CADILLAC CROWN ROYALE LANDAULET - Here's a view of the business end of a 1964 Superior-Cadillac Crown Royale Landaulet. Note the rounded rear quarter windows and distinctive trim on the rear door and fenders. This three-way side servicing funeral coach wears black sidewall tires - a relative rarity even on hearses.

1964 SUPERIOR-PONTIAC LANDAULET FUNERAL COACH - Superior's lower-priced Pontiac funeral coaches and ambulances were every bit as good-looking as their more expensive Cadillac companions. This handsome Landaulet Funeral Coach is a case in point. Side servicing was not available on the lower-priced Pontiacs. A standard wheelbase Superior-Pontiac Consort Landaulet was also available.

1964 MILLER-METEOR CADILLAC CLASSIC LIMOUSINE COMBINATION - Half of the professional cars built in the U.S. at this time were dual-purpose combination funeral cars and ambulances. This is a typical Combination Coach of the mid-1960s. Combinations were usually painted neutral colors (such as the white seen here). Note the Federal Model 17 Beacon Ray on the roof, the removable valance-type window draperies, and the emblem on the broad "D" pillar.

1965 S&S CADILLAC VICTORIA SIDE-SERVICING LANDAU FUNERAL COACH - Hess and Eisenhardt's most prestigious funeral coach was still the stately S&S Victoria. Originally introduced in 1938, the Victoria featured a richly grained padded leather roof. Note how the side door opening extends into the roof, and the Cycas leaf emblems in the triangular shield behind the side doors. This S&S has swag-type draperies instead of S&S' traditional airline type draperies.

1965 S&S CADILLAC FLOWER CAR - Hess & Eisenhardt built far fewer flower cars than rivals Superior and Miller-Meteor. Most S&S flower cars were, in fact, virtually custom-built. This imposing 1965 S&S utilizes commercial glass instead of standard passenger car glass. Note the large cab and stainless steel flower deck.

1965 SUPERIOR-CADILLAC SOVEREIGN LIMOUSINE FUNERAL COACH - Superior's fresh 1965 styling included an attractive "Tiara" roof treatment. In addition to the forward-angled "C" pillar, a chrome molding encircled the rear portion of the roof. All 1965 Superior, S&S, and Miller-Meteor Cadillac professional cars were built on Cadillac's new 158-inch wheelbase perimeter-frame commercial chassis.

1965 SUPERIOR-PONTIAC LANDAULET FUNERAL COACH - Superior's moderately priced Pontiac professional cars also got all-new styling this year. The top-line Landaulet was particularly attractive with its rakishly angled "C" pillar and smartly creased rear roofline. The companion Superior-Pontiac Consort Landaulet was equally good-looking.

1966 SUPERIOR-CADILLAC ROYALE LIMOUSINE COMBINATION - This is the prototypical American combination coach - classic limousine styling with folding attendant seats and two-piece airline style drapes. All that's missing is the demountable roof light. Note the air conditioning intake on the rear fender.

1966 SUPERIOR-CADILLAC FUNERAL COACHES - This factory photo shows two 1966 Superior-Cadillacs. The coach in the foreground is the Crown Royale Landaulet. The car in the background is a Crown Sovereign Limousine. Both feature up-and-over roof moldings. Note the Crown Royale emblem just behind the rear side door, and the extruded aluminum trim on the lower rear fenders.

1967 MILLER-METEOR CADILLAC EMBASSY FLOWER CAR - Owned by New Hampshire funeral director and Professional Car Society Past President Carlton Ham, this gorgeous 1967 Miller-Meteor Cadillac Embassy Flower Car is a familiar participant at PCS meets held in the northeast. The black crinkle top contrasts nicely with the Inverness Green body color and the gleaming stainless steel flower deck. Miller-Meteor built its last flower car in 1970.

1967 SUPERIOR-CADILLAC CROWN ROYALE LANDAULET - The crucifix mounted in the side window of this Superior-Cadillac Crown Royale Landaulet indicates that it was used by a firm which conducted Roman Catholic funerals. The small side marker lights on the front and rear fenders reveal that this hearse was built for a Canadian customer.

1967 SUPERIOR-PONTIAC CONSORT COMBINATION - Superior's standard wheelbase Consort continued to do well against such worthy competitors as Wayne Corporation's short-wheelbase Cotner/Bevington Oldsmobile Seville. This stock Superior-Pontiac Consort Combination was photographed in front of Superior's Southern Division plant in Kosiusko, MS, where all Superior-Pontiacs were built.

1968 SUPERIOR-CADILLAC CROWN SOVEREIGN LIMOUSINE - Premium features on this top-line Superior-Cadillac Crown Sovereign Limousine include the up-and-over roof molding, special trim on the lower rear fenders, and full-formal swag-type window drapes. The partition between the front and rear compartments and the air conditioning scoop on the rear fender indicates that this luxurious coach is a combination funeral car and ambulance.

100

1968 SUPERIOR-CADILLAC SOVEREIGN LANDAULET FUNERAL COACH - The lowest-priced Cadillac in Superior's extensive product line was the Sovereign. This classic landau hearse had closed rear quarters and a stylish, forward-angled B-pillar. This handsome coach was a straight end-loader.

1968 SUPERIOR-PONTIAC LANDAULET FUNERAL COACH - Superior's moderately priced Pontiac landau hearse was now also available with Sovereign styling; there were no quarter windows in the upper rear quarters. Three-way side servicing was not available in the moderately priced Superior-Pontiac hearses.

1969 SUPERIOR-CADILLAC CROWN SOVEREIGN LANDAULET - The Superior Coach Corporation was sold to the Sheller-Globe conglomerate in 1968. All 1969 Superior landau funeral coaches got the new style landau bow with straight ends as shown on this top-line Crown Sovereign. The formal roof styling introduced in 1965 continued for yet another year.

1970 MILLER-METEOR CADILLAC LANDAU TRADITIONAL - Miller-Meteor's standard landau funeral coach was called the Landau Traditional. This straight end-loading landau hearse was built for the Marcotte Funeral Homes of Windsor, Ontario. The author photographed it shortly after it was delivered. Miller-Meteor had introduced this sharp-edged body design in 1963.

1970 SUPERIOR-CADILLAC SOVEREIGN LANDAULET COMBINATION - Here's a classic combination funeral coach/ambulance in funeral service dress. The landau panels in the rear window openings were removed when the coach was pressed into service as an ambulance. Other combination features include the Federal Beacon Ray light on the roof and airline-type window draperies.

1970 SUPERIOR-PONTIAC LIMOUSINE FUNERAL COACH - The majority of the long and short-wheelbase Pontiac professional cars which rolled out of the company's Southern Division plant in Kosiusko, MS, were combinations. Limousine style straight hearses like this one were relatively rare. This 1970 Superior-Pontiac limousine style hearse has full formal draperies. Note the crucifix mounted in the rear side window.

1971 SUPERIOR-CADILLAC CROWN SOVEREIGN LANDAULET - This was a year of major styling change for Superior. Not only was Cadillac's commercial chassis redesigned, Superior restyled its Cadillac funeral coach and ambulance bodies for the first time since 1965. This is the top-line Crown Sovereign Landaulet, which retained the up-and-over roof molding originally introduced back in 1959.

1971 SUPERIOR-CADILLAC SOVEREIGN REGENCY LIMOUSINE FUNERAL CAR - Deliveries of Superior's extensively redesigned 1971 models were delayed for several months by a prolonged strike at General Motors. Production did not hit full stride until the first quarter of 1971. The new Sovereign Regency Limousine Funeral Coach combined landau styling with the long, low look of a limousine.

1971 SUPERIOR-CADILLAC FLOWER CAR - Superior's Cadillac Flower Car also got its first restyling since 1965. The new look included wide sail panels ornamented with chrome-plated landau irons. Note how the black crinkle roof finish extends to the upper rear body sides below the stainless steel flower deck. Built for a livery service, this flower car sports a two-way radio antenna on its roof.

1972 SUPERIOR-CADILLAC CROWN LIMITED LANDAULET - Introduced in 1970, the stately Crown Limited remained Superior's most exclusive (and expensive) hearse. Note the gracefully curved landau bow and the wreath ornament on the lower rear door. This is a straight end-loading funeral coach.

1972 SUPERIOR-CADILLAC CROWN SOVEREIGN LIMOUSINE COMBINATION - Superior's most prestigious models were still available as dual-purpose combinations. The addition of ambulance equipment and demountable warning lights instantly converted this coach from a dignified funeral car to an emergency ambulance. The wide up-and-over roof molding imparts distinction to the rear roof area, including the second side window.

1972 SUPERIOR-PONTIAC SOVEREIGN COMBINATION - Along with their big brother Cadillacs, Superior's lower-priced Pontiacs also got fresh, new styling in 1971. This is a 1972 Superior-Pontiac Sovereign Limousine Combination Funeral Coach and Ambulance. Note the airline type drapes, the removable landau panels in the rear side windows, and the air conditioning inlet on the rear fender. Superior-Pontiacs of this design were built through the 1975 model year.

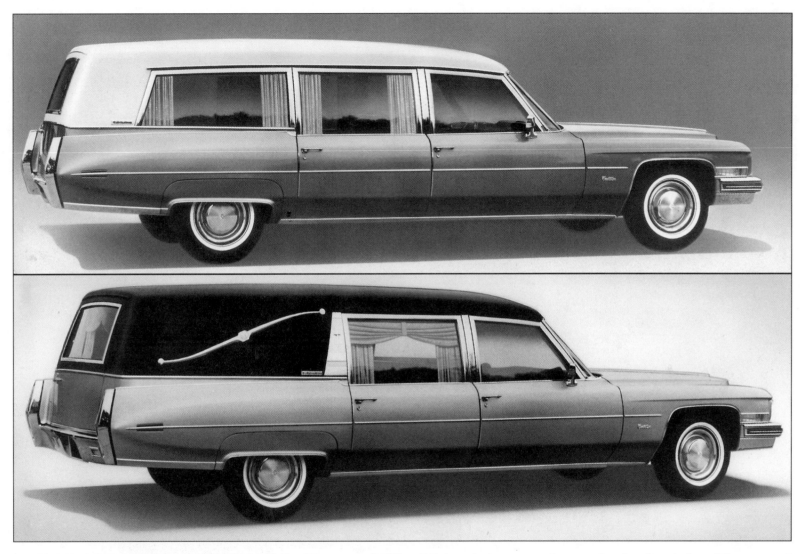

1973 MILLER-METEOR CADILLACS - Here are Miller-Meteor's two most popular body styles. The car at the top is the Classic Limousine Combination. The one below is Miller-Meteor's Landau Traditional Funeral Coach. Like all 1973 Cadillacs, the Series 69890 commercial chassis was equipped with GM's new energy-absorbing front bumper.

1973 COTNER/BEVINGTON OLDSMOBILES - Now a division of Miller-Meteor, Cotner/Bevington offered two sizes of professional cars on Oldsmobile chassis. Above is the short-wheelbase C/B Oldsmobile Seville Landau. Below is the long-wheelbase C/B Oldsmobile Cotington Limousine Combination.

1974 MILLER-METEOR CADILLAC ETERNA FUNERAL COACH - Introduced four years earlier, this Miller-Meteor body style combined the best of two worlds - the long, open look of the classic limousine and the formality of the traditional landau. Note the distinctive rear roof area and the tasseled drapes in the side windows.

1974 McCLAIN CADILLAC FLOWER CAR - An old, well-established funeral coach and ambulance distributor, McClain Leasing of Anderson, IN, built and sold a sizable number of attractive flower car conversions of standard Cadillac passenger cars. Co-author Tom McPherson photographed this factory demonstrator in a cemetery in Kitchener, Ontario.

1975 MILLER-METEOR CADILLAC CITATION LANDAU FUNERAL COACH - Miller-Meteor offered America's funeral directors no fewer than three premium landau-style funeral coaches on the Cadillac commercial chassis. In addition to the Citation shown here, M/M also offered an Olympian and the wood-grained Crestwood, all with their own distinctive roof treatments.

1975 S&S CADILLAC VICTORIA LANDAU FUNERAL COACH - Thirty-seven years after its introduction in 1938, Hess & Eisenhardt's premium funeral coach was still the prestigious S&S Victoria. This classic landau hearse featured a long-grain, padded leather roof and color-keyed landau bows. Note the formal window draperies and the wood-grained trim panel behind the rear side window. S&S marked its 100th Anniversary the following year.

1976 SUPERIOR-CADILLAC SOVEREIGN REGAL LANDAULET FUNERAL COACH - This would be the final year for the traditional full-sized professional car. The 1977 models were drastically downsized. Cadillac's 1975-1976 commercial chassis was powered by a 500 cubic inch V-8 engine. Superior, Miller-Meteor and S&S sales skyrocketed as funeral directors and ambulance operators stocked up on "the last of the BIG ones."

119

1976 MILLER-METEOR CRESTWOOD LANDAU FUNERAL COACH - In 1956 Meteor introduced a bold, new concept in hearse color schemes. The Meteor Crestwood had simulated wood-grain sides. The merged Miller-Meteor offered the Crestwood for 1957 and 1958 but there were few takers. The Crestwood name was revived on a new topline 1975 Miller-Meteor Landau. The 1975-1976 Crestwood had a woodgrain band around the rear half of the car.

1976 SUPERIOR-BUICK CUSTOM LANDAU FUNERAL COACH - After a 22-year production run, Superior discontinued its Pontiac professional car line at the end of the 1975 model year. To fill the gap left by the disappearance of its moderately priced Pontiacs, Superior introduced a new line of Buick-based hearses. These Buick Estate Wagon conversions were built for Superior by Armbruster/Stageway of Fort Smith, AR.

1977 S&S CADILLAC VICTORIA LANDAU - The U.S. professional car industry underwent a major transformation in 1977. To meet new federal fuel economy standards, General Motors "downsized" its full-sized cars. Cadillac's 1977 commercial chassis was significantly shorter and lighter than the one it replaced. To make matters worse, new ambulance regulations all but outlawed the combination. The curtain was also coming down on the passenger car-based ambulance. The effect of this downsizing was devastating. Hess & Eisenhardt was hardest hit; there was only one S&S body style for 1977, the Victoria Landau. This one, with optional oval coach window, was owned by the Hassebroek Funeral Home of Sullivan, MO.

1978 SUPERIOR-CADILLAC SOVEREIGN LIMOUSINE FUNERAL COACH - All three of America's principal funeral coach and ambulance manufacturers - Superior, Miller-Meteor, and S&S - downsized their products for 1977. The sudden demise of the passenger car-based ambulance and the dual-purpose combination sharply reduced demand for limousine styling. Only Miller-Meteor and Superior still offered limousine styling.

1979 S&S CADILLAC VICTORIA FUNERAL COACH - With the federally-mandated downsizing of its products in 1977, Hess & Eisenhardt offered only one hearse body style, the Victoria Landau. The company had built its last side-servicing hearses in 1976. After more than a century in business, Hess & Eisenhardt sold its S&S professional car division to rival Superior in 1981.

124

1979 AHA LINCOLN FUNERAL COACH - The U.S. funeral coach industry in the late 1970s underwent its most turbulent upheaval since the auto replaced the horse. Miller-Meteor went out of business at the end of the 1979 model year. Industry giant Superior was faltering and was sold off in 1980, and Hess & Eisenhardt (S&S) was soon also sold. This left the door open for a host of new conversion builders. One of these was AHA of Toronto, Ontario, which introduced a line of hearses on stretched Lincoln Continental chassis. AHA evolved into the Eureka Coach Company in 1981.

1980 SUPERIOR-CADILLAC CROWN SOVEREIGN LANDAULET - For the first time in three years the Cadillac commercial chassis was restyled for 1980. With only minor changes, this chassis soldiered on for another 12 years - the next major redesign did not appear until 1993! This 1980 Superior-Cadillac Crown Sovereign End-Servicing Landaulet was used by the Hulse & Playfair Funeral Home of Ottawa, Ontario.

More Titles from Iconografix:

*This product is sold under license from Mack Trucks, Inc. Mack is a registered Trademark of Mack Trucks, Inc. All rights reserved.

All Iconografix books are available from direct mail specialty book dealers and bookstores worldwide, or can be ordered from the publisher. For book trade and distribution information or to add your name to our mailing list contact:
Iconografix, PO Box 446, Hudson, Wisconsin, 54016 Telephone: (715) 381-9755, (800) 289-3504 (USA), Fax: (715) 381-9756

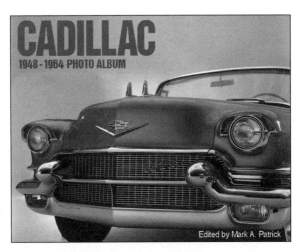

CLASSIC AMERICAN AMBULANCES
1900 - 1979 PHOTO ARCHIVE

Walt McCall & Tom McPherson

MORE GREAT BOOKS FROM ICONOGRAFIX

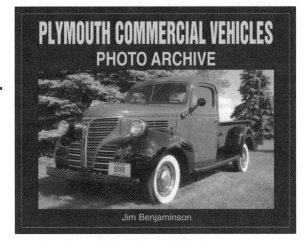

PLYMOUTH COMMERCIAL VEHICLES
PHOTO ARCHIVE

Jim Benjaminson

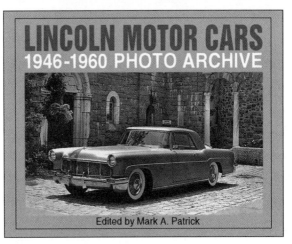

CADILLAC
1948-1964 PHOTO ALBUM

Edited by Mark A. Patrick

FIRE CHIEF CARS
1900 - 1997 PHOTO ALBUM

Donald F. Wood
W. Wayne Sorensen

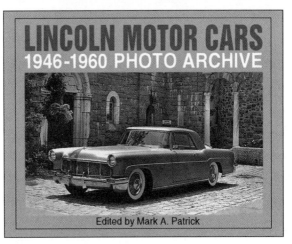

LINCOLN MOTOR CARS
1946-1960 PHOTO ARCHIVE

Edited by Mark A. Patrick

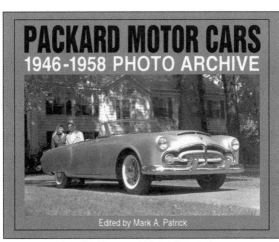

PACKARD MOTOR CARS
1946-1958 PHOTO ARCHIVE

Edited by Mark A. Patrick

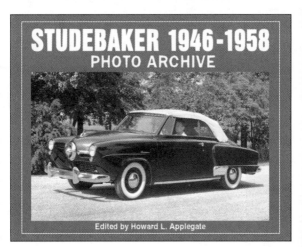

STUDEBAKER 1946-1958
PHOTO ARCHIVE

Edited by Howard L. Applegate